Knife on Snow

Knife on Snow

by

Alice Major

TURNSTONE PRESS

Turnstone Press gratefully acknowledges the assistance of the Canada Council
for the Arts, the Manitoba Arts Council, the Government of Canada through
the Canada Book Fund, and the Province of Manitoba through the Book
Publishing Tax Credit and the Book Publisher Marketing Assistance Program.

Printed and bound in Canada.

Library and Archives Canada Cataloguing in Publication

Title: Knife on snow / Alice Major.
Names: Major, Alice, 1949- author.
Description: Poems.
Identifiers: Canadiana (print) 20230191258 | Canadiana (ebook) 20230191282 |
    ISBN 9780888017680 (softcover) | ISBN 9780888017697 (EPUB) | ISBN
9780888017703 (PDF)
Classification: LCC PS8576.A515 K65 2023 | DDC C811/.54—dc23

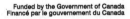

For all my nieces and nephews:
Colin Evans, Matthew Ellis, William Carter, Alasdair Carter,
Rachel Major, and Danielle Major

With love
and hope for all the future generations

And in memory of my dear niece Monica Ellis

"[A]s if there was a fate over people for fire."
—Samuel Pepys
recording in the aftermath of the
Great Fire of London, 1666

"And, as it was now allowed without hindrance, everyone who professed a knowledge of divination ... [was] permitted to question the oracles and the entrails, which sometimes disclose the future .... "
—Ammianus Marcellinus
writing his history of the later Roman Empire
at the end of the 4th century CE

"Mortichnium: The trail or trace left by a dying animal, especially as preserved in a fossil."
—Wiktionary

Contents

Travels in the solar system

Knife on Snow

End times 1:
Record of pressure

The plate tectonics of aging.
My right-hand middle finger points
north by northwest,
     a warping of the joint
from long pressure of a pen held
against it, squeezing out words.

Under my thinning crust,
the gradual thrust
     of shape-shifting time.
My hips now misaligned plates
like cratons, sections
     of ancient basement rock
stable over ages, while tendons
rift and rip around them.

It's been happening all my life,
this record of pressure, of matter
rising up, turning over,
eventually to be subsumed,
folded back into mantle—a slow,
continuous apocalypse.

A fate for fire

A fate for fire

once more a monster   moved through the night
a raging flame-dragon   ruled in darkness
fire-grim guardian   of a great treasure-mound
—Beowulf

1.

Dawn came then.   Dark dragged its grey tail
from sky's flat surface   and citizens woke
to no blue summer.   Their burning eyes
opened on orange,   an awful light,
fire-breath blown   from boreal blazing
to west and north,   wildfires ignited.

On fume-drugged highways   a car drives on.
Hours it has passed   under this pall
flanked by fields,   enfolded in hills.
High overhead,   on heaven's wide hill,
the sun walks   its way westward,
but its light casts no shadows.   A lurid lens,
smoke-filter,   saps colour.
Though green remains,   virescent glow
weird, intense,   world-end light.

This haze comes harried   over high mountains
from swathes of forest.   Scorched terrains,
another year,   the annual battle.
Like the dragon disturbed   in its treasure-den
that finds itself robbed,   ravages forth

again and again, unending rage.
                    Now forests flare
season after season in summer heats
as continents consume themselves.

The driver drives on through day-long dusk.
Remote from here, across the Rockies,
crews hack clearings in cruel heat.
Trees are torches, terrible angels,
crests of flame. This is crown fire—
fastest, most fierce. Flames leap
dangerous distances, devour timber.
Bale-fire, beast-fanged,
consumes creatures. Their corpses lie
chase-victims, charred in smoke.
Moose, mule deer, pine marten, bison—
no creature outruns such enormity.

> We followed fire, we hominins, traced its quick brush
> of flame over savannah to feast on its sweet detritus—
> roasted meat from smaller creatures trapped by heat.
> Like nighthawks foraging in a dragon's wake, we were
> hunters of the burnt.

2.

Here is a tale   that hall-thanes told
of wildfire and hubris   wound together,
when Thor and Loki   learned their limits.
Those gods journeyed   to the giants' home,
Jötunheim,   with its yawning hall.
Here Loki boasted   he'd beat their best
at gobbling down food.   And greedily raced
against the opponent   opening jaws
at the table's far end—   a trough piled high
with charbroiled flesh.   The rivals chowed down,
and met at last   at the massive tray's middle.
Loki stripped ribs,   licked off all gristle.
But the other had eaten   everything—
rib-bones, back-bones,   bare wood itself.
Loki had lost,   his loud mouth humbled.

Thor fails also,   strangely foiled
by the challenge he's offered,   a chore for a child:
to lift the cat!   A big grey creature
that stretches and stretches   like coiled string.
Thor tugs and toils   at this strange task,
but one paw only   can he pull from the floor.

The giant-king,   Jötunheim's lord,
escorts his guests,   these bumptious gods,
past the portcullis,   off the property.
In wrath and scorn,   the ruler reveals

his own ingenuity—   the eye-illusions
he conjured up   to conceal the truth:

"Loki encountered   no common opponent
in those teeth that chewed   at the table's far end.
He met wildfire itself.   Wildfire won.
Loosed on the world   it always will.

"You, Thor, hoisted   no household pet
but the Midgard Serpent   that circles the Earth
tail-in-mouth   and holds together
the sea-girded world.   You almost succeeded
in pulling apart   earth's primary bond.

"On your way   back to Asgard!
And don't come back,   you dangerous beings,
impetuous lordlings   who imperil Utgard."

> *We helped sculpt savannah, we pyrophilics, making*
> *ourselves small gods of flame. In our fire-stick*
> *footsteps, grasses sprang up, and berry bushes. Game*
> *gathered near. Our babies ate well. We learned to burn*
> *a landscape even before we thought to build a hearth.*

3.

Another summer   of thirst-season,
Canada's west   wilting, threatened
by the fire-beast rampant,   roused from sleep
after dry winter.   Drought's parched tongue
sucking at soil.   Spring too soon,
too sudden-hot.   Streams sinking,
roots wretched.   Rusted grass
and brittle shrubs   ready to burn.

Such was the scene   stretching beneath
the helitack crew   called to a blaze
near Fort McMurray—   city gripped
in the fist of forest.   Far-north Alberta,
oil-built town   on the Athabasca.

In former times   the first peoples
knew bitumen seeped   from the black banks,
patched travel-boats   with its dark tar.
Now hydraulic shovels   and heavy haulers
rip overburden   from buried oil sand.
Massive projects   ring McMurray,
scrape the boreal   down to its bones:
Jackpine and Steepbank,   the giant pits
of Muskeg River,   Mildred Lake,
Horizon Mine.   Heavy equipment
patrols pit-floors   where old petroleum
binds silica sand—   a sticky sea

where forest crowds   construction camps
and paycheques float   on pipelines' fate.

The copter pilot   keeps panic back
as smoke columns   swirl skyward,
shouts through the roar   of rotor blades,
Whoa! This is bad.
                No "one-tree wonder"
to curb with their bucket.   The canvas cistern
slung below   the chopper's stomach
is less than a mouthful   of meagre spit
at that fiery face.   Fury
has birthed itself,   beast out of bondage
growing greedy.   Winds gust,
drive destruction   to the city's door.

Only nine miles off,   in the angle of streams
(the water-web   that weaves muskeg:
Hangingstone,   Horse River
Saline Creek,   Clearwater)
homes cluster   in the clutch of trees
near a thin thread: a three-hundred-mile
strand of asphalt,   single escape route
south to safety.
                Days of siege then.
The beast stretches paws   into the city
again and again.   Embers swirl
across Athabasca—   astonishing leap!
The mile-wide river   can not repulse

fire's weather-wind.   Its wings spread
like a black bat's,   beast with a brain
circling the city,   seeking prey.

A morning's respite,   momentary.
A crust of cold air   contains the blaze.
Blue sky, false calm.   Birds know better,
fly in a frenzy,   fierce shrieks.
Then citizens see   the smoke-wall shift,
lean in on the town,   a louring tower,
orange-streaked ribcage.   Orders at last:
Evacuate! Every one.
Ninety thousand   now in flight
through the choked throat   and thick smoke
of that one road out,   walls of fire
on either hand.   Hell-mile, hellscape—
vehicles draining   through a downpour of flame,
raining embers,   the roaring lungs
of flames fifty feet high.   Fire-whirls of dust.

Scenes snatched   from thick smoke
beyond car windows: Kids on horseback
running their mounts   to uncertain refuge
past flame-walls.   Flash of police lights.
Cars stop   to scoop up dogs,
load them aboard.   Power lines
erupt in sparks.   Truck swirls to a stop
at a burning fence   (first blazing bite
at a loved home).   Heavy-loader

kicks into action,   flattens the fence,
races off,   ripping respite
from the beast's   big mouth.

Meanwhile, the monster   makes its weather.
Perilous updrafts   lift pyrocumulus—
that cloud-fist,   inferno's club—
into the air.   Arrow-flickers
of dry lightning,   but no downpour follows,
no rain-relief.   Only the roil
of Thor's thunder   thrashing the landscape
with a hazardous hail,   hot ember-seeds
that sprout new shoots.   Fire's spawn spreads
ever further   into green forest.

And the long road   logjammed
with crawling trucks,   creeping cars.
Drivers gaze   at dropping gauges,
emptying tanks.
                        How ironic!
Stranded for fuel   in forest terrain
that floats on petroleum.   This fragile thread—
the one route out,   the one-horsed
engine of economy—   all encircled
by boreal forest   designed to burn.

Plants build their green bodies with carbon, and the planet hoards those bodies after death. In the clasp of oceans, in the stone sarcophagi layered over drained, ancient seas, in stuck peat below permafrost.

So the dragon holds its treasure to its chest.

4.

Yet another year   of yellowed skies
and the dragon roused.   Now the driver
has left her car   at an airport lot
in her prairie town,   becomes passenger
over ocean.

Iceland approaches   at the aircraft's wing tip—
a low land   lifting itself
just clear of sea.   Coast enclosed
by a white scrim,   whipped-foam scribble.

Heathland below   heather-hued, spreads
into purple-dun distance.   The plane drops
to airstrip's arrow,   imposed stripe,
straight line laid   on hummocked landscape.

To the passenger   plane-enclosed,
the land below   looks lunar, alien.
Twelve centuries ago,   sailors roved
and settled here   near Smoke Cove.
Reykjavik—   remote shore named
for the steam breathed   from nearby springs,
magma's heat   escaping Earth's mantle.

This fire-formed land,   lava-layered,
where Earth's plates pull   at the planet's crust.
Fracture zones, fault lines.   Fissure swarms
crack patterns   like crazed porcelain.

Cooling now.   Its cliffs are castles,
staging grounds,   breeding sites
for migrating birds.   In millions they come,
the far travellers: slim phalarope,
Atlantic puffin.   Arctic tern—
that wide-winged   world wanderer.
Sea eagle.   Dabbling snipe,
wader of wetlands.   The welcome call
of golden plover,   promissory note,
sweet spring herald   that sings away snow.

And always, ravens.   Air's emissaries,
Odin's birds   bearers of news
returning to town   for winter's dark tale.
(If a raven permits   your touch on its plumage
it will whisper   some secret word
concerning your future.)

Colonists found   a country of trees,
wild birch thickets,   tea-leaved willow.
Forest filled   a fourth of that land.
No longer.   This landscape now
is low-growing: lichen and moss,
sheep sorrel,   shrubby cover.
The settler-surge   soon cleared
arable land.   Grazing livestock,
timber barns—   all the twined needs
of hungry humans   that hew down trunks.
That green canopy   did not grow back.

The passenger   picks her way
through Keflavik's   close-crowded aisles.
The airport's acres   now staging area
for new migrations.   Ten million a year
pass through this place.   Laden planes
touching down   from the terns' realm.
Now the birds' road   roars with metal,
soot and particulates,   unlocked sulfates,
high-sky contrails.   And carbon, of course:
jets' shed guano   joining the air.

> *We must burn to move. The slow combustion of*
> *lungs. The fast slash of engines across continents. The*
> *constantly increasing pour of dragons' breath into the*
> *protective shell of air.*

5.

Another tale   was told here
in far-off times,   in the firelit halls
of Iceland's   earliest settlers,
and preserved by a poet   who compiled lore
from a pagan world,   then passing away.
Snorri Sturluson,   that learned scribe,
wove a web   from old word-hoards:

Baldr the beautiful   bright as white nights
of the north's summer.   Second son
of Odin All-father   and dearest of all
Asgard's beings,   those quarrelsome Aesir.

But Baldr's rest   was besieged by dreams,
nightmares portending   peril, death.
His comrades all   took counsel together,
resolved to secure   Baldr's safety.
Frigg travelled far,   forest to sea,
took oaths from all   of Earth's beings
to spare her son.   Serpent and stone,
beasts and birds,   burning flame, water,
iron and metal   of every kind—
all vowed to her   never to harm him.

One thing only   Frigg overlooked—
a slender tree,   too small for threat.
But Loki learned   that lack of bond
and made of that tree   a trim spear.

From mischief or malice
he placed that shaft in the trustful fist
of a blind bystander, and directed his blow.
Hoder hurled it. The tip hit the mark
and Baldr lay dead. Weeping broke
from all the Aesir assembled there.
That violent death of one they deemed
unharmable hit at their core.
Their bright one gone!
                            They bore his body
to the shore's shingle where his great ship
waited by waves at the world's edge.
They piled his pyre on its high-planked deck
to send him burning to the sea's heart.

Now the Aesir found all their efforts fail,
their purpose broken with Baldr's death.
For all their sweat the ship would not stir.
They called at last on the cosmic force
of Jötunheim: they sent for a giant—
the woman Hyrrokkin, "Withered by Smoke."
She came to the ship by the sea's shallows,
its belly laid on timber logs,
and set her shoulder. *Ringhorn* shuddered
at Hyrrokkin's first pull; the heavy prow
released its grip, rushed down the rollers.

Wood flashed into flame   faster than thought:
the troubled ground   trembled and quaked
at Hyrrokkin's power.

After their loss,   the Aesir attempted
revenge on Loki,   bound his ribs
with his own son's entrails.   Enmity cannot
reach deeper.   No good result
could come of that   calamitous spark.
Giants came then   from Utgard's chaos—
those out-yards greater   than gods or men.
The ruinous road   to Ragnarok
commences then,   the coming Wyrd.

Flame is the spear-tip of change. A cusp is reached, the
dragon wakes. Tinder catches and the forest roars to
devouring life.

6.

The plane has crossed   the crown of ice,
that circumpolar   seal of snow
guarding the globe   with glacier and tundra
rimmed by forest—   the boreal's wreathe
of pine and spruce.
                              The passenger
stares down   as the plane descends
towards her home.   She has travelled
four thousand miles   in fourteen hours.
Europe behind,   where cities bake
and forests kindle   across Scandinavia.
She's relieved   to be returning
to her safe home.   But a strange shroud
surrounds the airport,   a sepia haze
spread over farmland   and stick-built suburbs.
Fire-retch   reaches horizon,
Hyrrokkin's breath   hovering for weeks.
Another season   of smoke, to signal
northern fire.

                    "One foot in the black,
one foot in the green,"   firefighters say
of the shifting line   they live on daily.

Grass fires roamed these plains, year after year. Fur traders blamed Indigenous people, but newcomers caused even more. A single gunshot could set land aflame. Settlers burned off grass to clear for crops, started new fires that raged out of control.

7.

As for the Aesir,   Asgard's heroes—
were they gods,   glorious denizens
of the unearthly?   Or only men?
Snorri's archive,   scholarly text
gleaned from old tales,   gave the gods
a human history: They were heroes
who had travelled   from Troy's plains,
their ancient home   in eastern realms.
Odin-led   and awe-inspiring,
they seemed divine   for goods they brought
and their fair faces,   foreign-hued.
Colonizers   they came at last
to reach their world's   northern rim,
sea-surrounded   Scandinavia.
That land's lords   allowed their entry,
welcomed the Aesir   as equals who bore
new tools and knowledge.   Those noble times
shifted in telling,   begetting tales
of cosmic beginnings,   made the Aesir gods.

Thus Snorri papered   the awkward seam
between old beliefs   and new bibles,
as he traversed   his own troubled time
of politics,   clan-peril,
sea-kings' conquest,   kidnap and fealty.

So, always,   are narrative's atoms
captured, sifted,   and recombined
in the never-ceasing   cycle of story.

> *A tale of today: Carbon dioxide hoards heat, its triad*
> *of atoms clasping a pinprick photon in their grasp. Its*
> *molecules make up a sliver of a sliver of the world's*
> *substance. How could a few more matter? Because in*
> *the vast numbers of the atomic realm, even a closetful*
> *of air contains more CO_2 molecules than there are stars*
> *in the visible universe.*

> *Tiny spears massing.*

8.

The woman moves   through world-change,
seeking direction,   both driver
and passenger—   part cause,
part witness of   earth's unwinding.

She feels   like the fugitive
in the skald's tale.   Escaping pursuit,
he creeps through   a narrow crevice,
discovers a hoard   of dragon-gold.
While the wyrm sleeps,   he steals a cup—
one small theft   of a precious thing—
and slips away   on stealthy feet.
He knows the ale-cup,   gem-encrusted,
will earn him mercy   from an angry lord
and scurries home,   safe for a time
from human doom.   But the dragon knows
its hoard's balance   to the smallest bead
and, roused, flies forth   in a fever of reckoning
to wreck the land   with ravage and flame
every dark night.   Destruction and death
blast that country   and blight its folk.
Thus we find   our fates are bound
by actions of others   wanting only
to save their skins.

So, the woman comes,   safe for now,
to her fort-city,   one foot in the green
of north's circle,   summer-gardened.
But smoke's portent   smudges the sky
and ravens are gyring.   The ravens speak only
among themselves—   thief-tales perhaps
but no clear word   of the world's future.

She considers   scraps recorded
from her continent's   complex past:
its restless massing,   migrations, treks
across its realms.   Creatures moving
like a single body,   one fluid being.
Huge shaggy herds: the hoof-shaking
Earth-pulse   as those old ones passed.
Sky-pulse   of passenger pigeons
streaming onward,   waves and waves,
line upon line,   limitless.

Billions they were,   birds and bison
shaping their world.   Keystone species
yoked to the whole   of their habitat—
the rise and fall   rhythm and stasis
of other life forms   lay with them.
And now they're gone.   That great gap
ripped by rifles   raised against
animal throngs   thought to be
inexhaustible   by the influx
of colonists   coming, careless,

each believing   he bore only
a harmless spear   against the whole
of the bright world's   beautiful body.

> *Plains burned in every direction. Blind bison*
> *wandering about, hair singed to the skin, skin*
> *shrivelled and burned, eyes swollen and closed fast.*
> *Stumbling, running foul of a large stone, tumbling*
> *downhill, falling into creeks.*
>
> *A hoard of living things laid waste.*

9.

The wind shifts,   shoves smoke aside,
summer's clear sky   asserts itself
with grass and growth.   The green world's
brilliant body   is beautiful still.
But ravens cry   in the false calm.
Fire keeps coming   closer to home
in the warming world,   a warning flash
of Surtur's sword   as cities reach
fattening fingers   deep into forest
and sparks fly   among ourselves.
Pudding Lane,   Paradise Valley.
Fort McMurray's   flame-razed homes.

And where do we go?   In London's Great Fire,
as panic flared,   the poor pigeons
were loath as people   to leave their homes
and beat their wings   at balconies, windows,
then fell to ground,   feathers flaming.

Our rare Earth   is being written:
metamorphic   stone-memory.
Sagas and skald-tales   a faint sediment
brushed on its surface,   breath-currency,
exchange of vapour.

What thin page   will be pressed here
into rocks' record?   What dark ribbon
of soot and ash   will inscribe itself—
black ink-stain,   baleful tale
of our great burning?

> Samuel Pepys got up at three a.m. when his servant
> called and went to look out the window to see glowing
> sky lit by the great London fire.
>
> "But, being unused to such fires as followed, I thought
> it far enough off; and so went to bed again, and
> to sleep."

End times 2:
I bear you company ...

... sitting beside you on this old sofa,
claw-scratched leather
you have curled on all these years.
Sunlight's silver-gilt shifts
like a watermark on your soft, soft fur.
You purr while I rub your tummy,
and with a small sigh-grumble
tuck your tail into sleep.

The late sun westers to the equinox
and I am filled with the god-
awful responsibility of knowledge,
its terrible asymmetry.

You purr and you are dying. But what
can you know of that? Not
that this day is appointed
for that stern necessity. We sit
in the sunlight on the skin
of other dead animals.
I cannot bear it, crave to be absolved,
your impossible forgiveness.

Knife on snow

Knife on snow

"These dangers ... I, a former soldier and a Greek,
have set forth to the measure of my ability ...."
—Ammianus Marcellinus, concluding his history of
the late Roman Empire, c. 393 CE

1.

Wicked wedge, its shape embossed
on the untracked snow-crust of my city yard.
Blade crusted with frost.
The sky is, as always, dark
at this early winter evening hour. There are
streetlights in the alley—glum sodium
burns like the light of dying stars.

     What arc of history
brings this here, so deep inside my property
surrounded by a wall of caragana
fifteen feet high. Dropped impossibly
like a god's random hammer
—a silent, unnerving thunderbolt.

Its anonymous menace.
The lack of explanation for its cold
and alien metal presence.
Irrational. Yet surely it called
for agency, intention, to fling the blade
this far. My hedges grow thick
and tangled.
     There must be rage

beyond my narrow bailiwick,
my guarded fiefdom in the snow.

This took one hell of a throw.

2.

I need to know its provenance.
What mysterious trajectory
aims this silver point at me?

The blade etched with a brand,
Weimar Steel, seared upon
its surface gleam. A name
dropped out of nowhere, echoing

a fragile republic spun out
of clouds—collapse, aspiration—
a temporary eyespot
in the circling weather of war.

And further echoes from the history
of weaponry and iron:
the dammed tributaries of the Rhine;
the Ruhr's reverberating thunder
beating artillery into being;
industrialists who steal the ear of emperors
and build an empire of steel.

The currents circling even deeper
through climate systems of conflict:
the infrasonic rumble of imperium.
Kaisers who mass troops on frontiers
and take their title from the Caesars.

3.

Cold clasps my shoulders.
I want to turn back to the lighted room
behind me, its haven built
of bookshelves, warmth, and words—
the past's accumulating legacy,
old voices murmuring from quiet pages.

Enter Ammianus Marcellinus,
soldier turned historian, witness
to disastrous campaigns and death.
One of the recorders who keep trying
to read the currents.

This empire is crumbling. Rome's enchained defence—
its line of forts forged along Gaul's rim—is rusting.

The Republic's white-arc glow, its legend of discipline,
its iron resistance to foes ringing the city

has long since blurred. The restless clans that raid its borders
   are now half-Roman in blood and armaments.

The whole continent surges with migration. Tribes
   pour from place to place, like liquid seeking level.

They want land or loot, conquest or a place to be at peace,
   escape from rulers or simply openness of fields.

Their tongues tangle. Bloodlines intermingle.
   They are the changing weather of the world.

And the emperors fail. They thrust up like thunderheads
   or blanket landscapes like sour, sea-borne fog.

Some golden ages: Pax Romana, summer stretches
   under scholar-kings, careful administrators.

But most are a series of troughs and ridges, storm fronts
   great or lesser in strength, to be watched and lived through.

Emperors of average merit, propelled by partisans,
   hiring claques to cheer their purple assumptions.

Emperors conspicuous for paranoia, listening to whispers
   behind every door, sending spies into the city.

Caesars seize power, sometimes share it, govern shifting fragments
of the ungovernable, die in their beds or by knife-gash.

Within a century, the long flood of Rome's empire in the west
will recede, like a storm surge driven far inland.

4.

This bitter winter night.
The city light that blanks the stars
and stares at the metal wedge
stamped on snow.
My small, staked territory.

I am here, another echo in the infrasound
of history: clanging kingships, twang of borders
snapping and reshaped. The fast clash of battle
                              speeds away, fades,
but its long, low, underlying wavelengths
propagate across oceans, carry force—
          the power assumed
to break bodies, push them aside.

My own folk, Celts, caught and tumbled
by the fierce inrush of war
and the tidal flats it leaves behind—

poverty, vassalage, fervent dreams.
Pushed to the far edge of Europe
then helping to push empires
over oceans. Even here, to this
northwest corner of a continent.

Through the silence of frost,
currents surge and crash
below my hearing. I bow my head,
weighted-down legatee
of empire.

5.

From my small room where the past is ranged
on shelves, as if it's over,
the words of Ammianus murmur on
about the emperor he served.

A spear-tip hurtled out of nowhere, flung into history
 by an unknown hand in a frantic melee

to slice the side of the Emperor Julian, part his ribs,
 and lodge in the soft jelly of his liver.

Julian had felt death coming. In dreams, Rome's Genius,
  a sad, veiled figure, stepped away through parted curtains.

Entrails of sacrificial animals were unsatisfactory,
  and a falling star shocked the sky with flailing brilliance.

He told his attendants he was destined to die here.
  The wound in his side gaped, its black blood flooded out

stranding his troops in hostile territory, like birds
  whirled up in a hurricane and left to struggle home.

Ammianus sums up Julian, sadly,

Neither corrupt nor cruel. Reckless to emulate
  heroic Alexander. Overly superstitious.

Still, he left peace in Gaul and did not start that Persian war.

Implicit in Ammianus's sad assessment:
  If only he had lived.

6.

Could change swing
on such small hinges?

That question bats
back and forth
like a door clapping
in a storm wind.
Can cusp or nudge
set fate's direction?
A javelin's random jab,
a meteor that rips
the sky's rib,
a butterfly's flapped wing—
and the world spins
differently from then.

But weather needs a world beyond the butterfly
—context, causes, complex predispositions.

Tilt of the planet's axis to slide air sideways,
twist air and water into spirals, Coriolis curls.
Heat and cold to rise and fall, shoulder each other
aside. Air pressures to clash and snarl
driven by difference.

Just as human history is a weather
stirring constantly in conflict's climate.

Anger the axis our species spins around,
our nature a wobbling ball
tilting season to season, eon to eon.
Interacting cycles that tow an atmosphere
in which we're all susceptible
molecules, compelled
to participate.

Landscapes claimed, colonized,
borders blurred by blood and burnings, blasts
of man-made armament, tanks massed,
rifle barrels and barrel chests
and borrowed time. Weapons rain,
the sky grows deadly.

All war is civil war,
internal to ourselves.

7.

I lift knife from snow-surface,
finger its frost-forged edge.
Could such a token
simply arrive from sky?
Could some corvid's claws
be strong and strange enough
to drop it here?

We always seek for portents
in the changing patterns of heaven.
But the hedge-rimmed patch of sky above me
will not communicate. Above the streetlight
no stars announce omens.

Ammianus warned against
the dangerous urge of superstition:
Stars don't fall. It's impious to think
the gods would toss their fixed stars down
like stones at a pigeon.

Still, he conceded,
there are patterns to observe:
We do not owe auspices and auguries
to the will of birds. They do not know
the future. But their flight is directed
by the powers above.

To those who properly observe
rite and ceremony, such phenomena
offer prophecy.

8.

Centuries ago, a star
seared across this whole territory—
iron lump of asteroid, screaming
brilliance, roaring to rest near the Battle River.

Child who fell from the sky, the people named it,
those who dwelled here long before the fences,
who watched the wild sky-streak and found
its landed hammer. Meteorite moulded
by the flowing heat of passage,
metal melted into smooth pits, ripples.
The warm liver-brown of ore
frosted with a faint net of silver

We ponder what it means, this object
in which some see a bison head, others
the contours of a human face or a landscape
of cliffs rising from the roll of prairie,
and I think of convolutions
in a human cortex.

We are all historians, recording past
to foretell inscrutable future.

Many said that its arrival meant
the land and buffalo belong to everyone,
should not be battled over. Some maintained
Creator had sent it as protection—

should it be taken, sickness and famine
would follow. (As they did
in the plundering centuries after settlers
poured onto these plains, stole
Manitou Asinîy away.)

Now the spirit rock waits
in a round room, ringed
by braids of sweetgrass,
fragments of offering.

It is iron forged
before iron was a weapon.

9.

But the hammered artifact I hold is human—
this blade locked into white thermoset plastic.
This blade with its German name
that might be made in China.
The whole world is involved in this,
our terrible, obstreperous times.

I have been sheltered
behind my tall, tough hedges, but now
feel stripped, unprotected, naked to the sky.

This toss of aggression
completes some series of purposeful acts
whose history I cannot know in full.

Anxious colonist, I lift my hands
seeking some other augury,
a message from the realms beyond anger,
some small omen of hope.

End times 3:
Bless my eyes

How I've taken you for granted,
hard-working contraption, camera obscura,
darkened chamber where light's beads
thread on a string of signals, linking me
to the world's weave, its moiré and rainbows,
its depths of field—
                    sheen of green and cobalt
in a magpie's wing. I have been your pupil
all these years.

Any camera would struggle
to render what you mirror seamlessly—
movement's constancy,
proliferating daylight, the startling sparkle
as I pass through snow.

Blessings on you. You get tired
at times. Close your lids for now. Rest
will come. Someday you won't even need
to show me dreams.

Dreams of anger

A dream of anger

In this dream, I revert
to the holding pen of childhood:
the basement flat, below grade, lit
by daylight smudged
like diluted halogen
through narrow window-slits.

I have quarrelled
with my sister, adolescents
in a hair-pulling, eye-scratching snap
of incipient estrogen

        then
I am walking down the dull hall
that leads to bedrooms. At its far end,
a plain, closed door
where a woman stands staring.
Ordinary, uncanny. Eyes
flat as stones.

Her stare will remain
locked on me
for decades after I awaken.

I know what she portends:
if I push past
that door's drab barrier,
           rage
will be limitless. Nothing will stem
its ruin. Anger will drag me
willy-nilly mare's tail
to nightmare's most furious,
bitter end.

Path integral

I'm angry about anger—this all-too-easy sheet of flame with
its ever-ready pilot light ready to sweep the brain. This coil
of neurobiology, the braided lash that rounds us up into
obedient legions to be hectored from lecterns: *They're taking
things away from you, those hidden elites, those threatening
other-coloured others!* This fetter fastened round our necks, a
convenient collar where demagogues can attach the leash.

I want to poke around inside the brain, unroll the
wrinkled cortex into a flat, creased sponge and map anger's
coordinates. Along the x-axis: half a billion years of animals
trying to survive by fighting back. Along the y-axis: the
logarithmic scale of primate generations, social structures
becoming as convoluted as a coral reef, anger rearing up
when others break the rules. And z, the dimension of the
individual life, its traumas and tender spots.

On this stretched-out cortex, I want to locate anger's many
domains—bile and choler, ire and indignation, revenge and
aggression—and trace the paths that chain them. Where is
the fury that is close to joy, its luxurious purity? Where do we
locate the sullen burn of grudge? Where do I find the domain
anger shares with religion, our gods of righteous wrath and
war with their foreheads of bronze or steel? Where is that
narrow territory where unnecessary rage roars up when I'm
hurt by something as minor as a stubbed toe?

Surely knowing this territory would help us negotiate these fragile, fractious times.

But the map bewilders me—the infinite calculation of its tangled functions, its derivatives. I can't compute the area covered by anger, the limits to which it might converge, nor the sum-over-histories of its evolving wave that rolls through brains and time and populations. I can't sum up this cortical compulsion that traps us, this power we hand over to noisy purveyors of conflict.

> *The dog flings itself barking*
> *wildly at the fence*
> *and its mirror dog beyond.*

Anger's arithmetic

one person shouting on the corner is a man
haunted by some demon

three on the corner become evangelical,
followers of a hollering God

five on the corner might be an audience,
puzzled but passive

seven on the corner could include the individual
who yells back
at the other six who block the sidewalk

eleven people on the corner
may bring signs—
divine-inspired directions

thirteen on the corner might
begin the straggle of parade
surge of concerted march

seventeen people leaving the corner
might begin the brouhaha of righteousness
pushing unbelievers to the side

nineteen people might become a mob
primed to lynch

leap on through escalating primes
until group becomes rabble
becomes riot

until one thousand and nine people could become
enough to storm a legislature
shouting to the god of freedom

yet this upsurge does not rise
simply through counting's primal stride
marching to a necessary sum

but from the math of tipping points,
the complicated calculus
of interaction

until the point is reached
where individuals become
less free, less individual,

a coordinated wave state
simplified into
acting as one

Alarums and excursions

August   civil twilight   the police helicopter
prowls and growls   a circling insect   long-bodied

lights crimson and emerald   on its stinging tail
like mating signals   warnings

warm air heavy   a stuffed cushion   supporting
the copter's mechanized whine

haze   a pinkness to everything
leftover wavelengths   from a red round sun
like a brilliant bullet hole   fired
at the sinking west

floating smoke   borne high
from distant forests   on fire
everything coming closer

we feel enclosed in rosy organza
wrapped   in a cell we can't escape
a world we can't get out of

continuous swish-roar
traffic's pink noise   punctuated
by sirens'   red-lipped whistle
and departing   Doppler drop

beyond the neighbourhood's
trees and rooftops   a downtown tower
lifts a thick finger   tall glass-sided monitor

topped with scarlet LEDs   signalling
danger

now voices rise   uncivil   shouts
disorderly noise   from a nearby street

urgent fragments   profanity
indistinguishable angers   breaking out

in emergency   break glass

Immune response

A bomb lobbed into the friendly room of an online seminar:
a fluttering, electronic whistle like someone searching rapidly
through radio bands, a voice inserted into opening greetings.
"Ma'am? Will someone get that n----- off the screen."

Tech host promptly disinfects, sends "John Smith" off
to circulate in the cyber-bloodstream beyond. Impotent
mischief, chortling and nursing his own little surge of
adrenalin and whatever long-term rage infects him. But we
are enraged.

And so he achieves his ambition—he has poured his anger
into us. Abominable contagion, that worser spirit. It goes
beyond racism, though racism is its pus-filled boil, the
proliferating buboes that signal circulation of disease. A
pandemic spread by a pathogen that knows us too well, has
evolved its cellular machinery along with ours, inserts its
spike protein into cells ready to nurse and breed it. Anger's
inflammatory response takes down the whole organism.

> *Anti-maskers march*
> *shouting against the regulation*
> *to cover your mouth.*

"Progressive"

Dusty spring, street-silt of winter dried
and flaring in our faces
like a powder blown to blind the populace
by some malign magician.

Across the street, banners flap
in the foehn-blast of chinook—
a protesting parade that shouts
and struggles against the gusts:
 "I heart Alberta oil and gas!"
"Take the brakes off
        oil sands development."
"Down with carbon taxes!"

Slogans that ignite the counter-fire
of my small group of pals,
environmentally aware and headed for lattes.
My kind, dear friend shakes her fist,
yells unexpected obscenities.

        Progressive, we style ourselves
as we head forward on our side
of the street, walking parallel
to that straggled, placard-waving gaggle.
For us they represent
the tailing-pond of history,
its wrong side.

And yet I am embarrassed
at claiming this grand arc of narrative.
Dust grits my eyelids
as weather-changing wind
blusters against our chests.
Along the asphalt expanse
that separates us, vehicles stall
and rev their engines at the stoplights
while all of us progress
in time's direction.

Be at peace

Be at peace! My mother's voice, remembered,
rattles back at rattling windowpanes.
Beyond them, the wind's wild tantrum
hurls its fists of snow
                on and on
like a child who has forgotten
how to stop.

That phrase, the voice of her, driven
to irritation's last ditch
at whatever had gone spinning
out of control. It meant, *Sit down.*
Shut up. Possess your soul
in patience.
          I hear it now,
want to yell it out myself—at trees
lashing fruitless branches, at snow
whirling into huddled faces, at the nations
piling up stupid ideologies,
childish hates.
            Sit down. Shut up. Cease
the noise. I want to snap
the spinning planet to attention
with that command's angry kindness:
       Be at peace!
Oh, let us be
     at peace.

The dream opens ...

... as dreams do, in a dark wood
on a road where trees push forward, pull back
in waves, and phantom branches brush the hood
    of the pickup truck I drive. (Me? Drive a truck?)
    In the rear-view mirror, a shrouded burden
    looms, sullen block on the pickup's deck.
The road widens to a clearing, cordoned
by a wooden arm that blocks the way ahead.
From the sentry box beside it, the warden
    steps out. She is young, stern, her blonde head
    official below a visor. She gestures
    to another track I have to take instead,
bending back into the wood, to its pressures
of shadowed savagery and mottled beasts,
to the poisonwood and nettles it sequesters.
    "You can't go farther here. *That* way." She speaks
    like well-trained iron. But a galvanizing
    force lifts, a coiled spring released.
"Oh yes I can," I say, surprising
even myself, and gun the gas.
The barrier dissolves like steam rising
    from a boiling pot. I hurtle past
    the turnoff to inferno, beyond
    the stifling forest and the holdfast
of old grudge-engendered bonds,
head towards exulting hills outlined
on open sky. Anger used and jettisoned.
    There are frontiers to cross, and leave behind.

End times 4:

"Your house might qualify for a heritage plaque"

says the flyer in my mailbox. So could I!
We've been here decades. But we're shy,
my house and I. Don't really want to advertise
our advancing age, our cracks and dips.
Still, I think I'd like a plaque.
I'd hang it on the iron laundry pole
out back. Its rust-brown spine
stands straight, rooted in the clay
that lay below the slough
that used to shine here. No longer tasked
with anchoring the drying flags
of laundry, it stands, cryptic,
like the entrance to a bygone land. Old,
and strangely proud of that.

The last Ediacarans

The last Ediacarans

Fossils from the Ediacaran era are found in a particular layer of sandstone around the globe—puzzling animals with no apparent descendants today. A specimen of one such creature, Yilingia spiciformis, *was found along with its mortichnium, the traces of its final movements.*

I. Sediment

So much world is coming
at me from screens. They blast
their coruscating pixels, simulcast
shreds of nonsense—like scraps
of disaggregating plastic that drift
downward through the water column.

I am drowning in distraction
like a fish feeding from that sift
of rotten pollen.
Useless inertia drifting past
to settle into sediment—
a mud that will outlast
our life forms, drying to a fossil cage,
delimiting an age.

2. *Yilingia spiciformis*

It crawls from stone, a jointed ribbon
as long as my hand, wide as my thumb.
Its soft-body armour and millipedal form
now infiltrated by minerals to become
fossil, along with the faint groove
dragged by its passage over Panthalassa's
tranquil sea floor of muddy sand.

This final track, preserved *mortichnium*,
(death's footprint) remains to prove
this was no plant frond or random strand
of floating protoanimal. Time engraved
the record of a creature that could move:
in *Yilingia's* shallow, stone-sealed trail
a trace of purpose has been saved.

3. Cap carbonate

Yilingia creeps towards its end-time
through mats of dying microbes.
Something is sucking oxygen
from ocean floors around the globe.
Sponge-soft mats of the simple-celled—
in which these last Ediacarans
burrow, feed, and leave their trails—
collapse implacably towards black shale.

The not-yet-worm crawls in not-yet-rock—
a muck of carbon and lifeless lime, a scum
that will compress to a thick ceiling
sealing off the old, azoic aeons
below. Border, limit, clear dividing line
between what's going, and a world to come.

4. Great Pacific Garbage Patch

A casual apocalypse of plastic,
the tossed-aside and lost—bags and bottle caps,
fishing nets, the beady foam of polystyrene cups.
Petrochemical debris is rounded up,
herded by the currents' cyclone churn,
and thrashed to fragments by the shredding sun.

A microplastic cloud that casts a pall
on autotrophs below—algae, plankton. Cells
that support themselves by chewing light,
and then support all other life in turn.

Polymer molecules, dense enough to sink,
drape a suffocating shawl
on all below. Anoxia creeps in
to strangle life in polyethylene.

5. End time

A mineral record of Ragnarok:
three billion years of upheaval
lie below this cap, layers of rock
hammered in archaic battles
between Frost Giants and the hot sons
of Muspell. Global glaciations
lose the long war against warmth.
Swings of atmosphere advance, pull back,
and plaster strata over seabed.

This stone lid formed around the fossils
of inexplicable animals—quilled fronds,
puzzling quilted bags, *Yilingia's* scuttle.
Then, above the lid, those life forms
end—everything stopped dead.

6. Cementation

I move through my dwelling-place,
this block of air below a ceiling
stippled with plaster, imagining the space
becoming rock, silt settled, paralysis
setting in. Beyond the window, cliffs
built higher and higher. Layered striations
recording life—what it absorbs, excretes.
How it alters, atom by atom, the sift
of chemistry through the planet's crust,
as time's enormous patience
alters life. Cell and shell, the dust
of bone and lignin—all constantly accrete
and harden.
              In my sedimentary basin
I feel claustrophobic, old, and stiff.

7. Tales of the apocalypse

We are frightened. We've told so many tales
of doomsday, deluge, cataclysm,
imminent end-times when angered deities
hit the cosmic reset button—quittance
for the wickedness and careless vandalism
perpetrated by our species. Now it feels
as though the reckoning of Ragnarok arrives
at our coastlines, havoc setting in.

And we know we've launched this ship ourselves,
Naglfar, built from humanity's own keratin
and dead detritus. This largest of all ships
will bring the fire giants into battle.

No wonder the young are shaking angry fists,
afraid the lid is coming down on us.

8. Time flows through history

The future comes at me in flakes
and raindrops—a sudden midnight rain
releasing drought. The relief of liquid
that takes its shape
        from where it finds itself.

Now: this moment that suspends
its translucent page between past
and future, like a flickering screen
on which the transient makes patterns
        that constantly reshape themselves.

Here is where I find myself, for now.
Beyond the windowpane, the garden's
cracked, compacted skin expands
and heals. While liquid time pours on
        and does not end.

9. Segmented body plan

Yilingia leaves clear evidence
of segmentation, a jointed chain
built from repeating elements—
trapezoidal plates, the same
recurring shape stuttered
over and over and over again.

An innovation frequently reprised:
it's the polymer principle,
adopted eagerly by animals
for building chitin, feather, fingernails,
and the genes immortalized
in DNA. Such chains make membranes
hard to tear or scratch. Insoluble
in water. Tough scraps that last.

10. *Ideonella sakaiensis*

The things that turn up in garbage dumps!

In a waste of plastic waste, a lipid capsule
evolves, an arriviste bacterium
inventing itself, squeezing out an enzyme
that can snip a wrapped-up molecule
of PET to unlock nourishment
from plastic's toxic, tangled twine
of carbon, oxygen and hydrogen—

                           those elements,
harmless in themselves, that we combine
into plastic's static, structured clumps
that temporarily seem eternal

until *Ideonella* and its microbe-kind
weave dissolution's necessary mesh
and save our living world from permanence.

11. After Ragnarok

Apocalypses tend to end with gardens,
the promise that the smoke of strife will clear,
the sea retreat from land and leave it fair
and fruitful. Life in the form of a human pair
will creep out from the heart of trees.

Of course, the old gods come through too,
like polymer units, macromolecules
we have invented and find difficult
to dissolve: the vengeful sons of Odin,
day-bright Baldr. They will seat themselves
on the empty field where Asgard gleamed
and find again the gods' gold gaming-pieces
to start the game anew—another run
at complex life, recurring Wyrd
of the accidental gods we have become.

12. Wormworld

So, start again. *Yilingia* is gone,
leaving no descendants, at the dead end
of a stone groove.
               Yet its thread of DNA
is wound into the long fuse burning
from Earth's earliest embryos
(cells assembled into replicating spheres)
to the panoply of animals that explodes
with the Cambrian.
               Just above the stern close
of the Ediacaran, comes a sea floor churning
with tiny tube worms—ecosystem engineers
that break their world down, stirring
its sediments, opening new space
where species effloresce into difference.

That age of industry left us a maze
of slender tunnels burrowing towards today.

13. This my mortichnium

It's the promise of apocalypse:
we shall not die, but we shall all be changed.

An offered hope: some future always slips
through the present's screen.

Filter-feeders—animals from krill
to whale—exist to sift and clean

whole oceans. Sediment encrypts
the past in scribbled tracks and bioglyphs.

The virtue of plastic is to be malleable
as well as stubborn in its written scripts.

From the torrent pouring on without me,
something will survive. A world will last.

And sometimes, in the stone-slow change to fossil,
our soft parts wear away but leave a cast.

End times 5:

Living with dinosaurs

        flutter of flute-notes and house finch flash
        of warm carmine

    whirrrr of pigeon wings

       ongoing sparrow natter
       the politics of flock

     a gull calls   again   again   again
invisible bird flying from one edge of the sky to the other
    mew   *mew*   *mew*   *mew*
     each call a stitch in the thread of passage
        trail of flight made visible
            by sound

(dinosaurs! we label
yammering, rufous-headed noisemakers
in their regressive nests
—such a slander on the animals,
cataclysm's survivors,
whose tuneful descendants
live with us every day)

       squawk says a magpie quietly
       from the roof of the garage next door

    croodle say the pigeons *hiccup hiccup croodle*

a chickadee lands on the ash tree branch
makes the smallest *plink*
     possible

Travels

in the solar system

"Planet Nine is out there," claim astronomers

The solar system's orbits are haunted by trauma. There was the protoplanetary disk, its spin synched to the sun's equator, rotating horizontally like a plate held on an expert waiter's hand. Eight planets coalesced from its material. But a ninth planet was flung aside by the gas giants, Jupiter and Saturn, their gravity firing it away like a stone from a slingshot. Now it circles far beyond the disk's original territory. It pulls the orbits of the other eight slightly askew, like peas whirling round a mildly tilted plane. But other bodies farther out, fragments in the Kuiper Belt, leftovers from the formation of the solar system, follow paths that are much more eccentric, upended by the slow and lasting residue of violence.

> *Consequences follow on and on.*
> *Insiders hardly notice. Impacts hit*
> *harder at the margins.*

Tiny collisions shape Mercury's atmosphere

Mercury is stuck to the sun, which moves slowly across her very long days. The solar disc is large in planet's sky, like an oversized computer screen planted on a desk. With difficulty she peels herself away from it to gaze for a while at the rest of the universe. But then she's back to staring at it for another long session—the constant coruscation of its corona, its flares and dark spots, its awful sameness.

Every sunrise, Mercury blows through a pepper-spray of micrometeoroids, fragments of blown-up comet. They're tiny, but they come blasting from the opposite direction to her own orbit—a harsh, insistent dust that scrubs molecules of magnesium and calcium from her surface and leaves them drifting in her tenuous air.

> *Morning. Social media*
> *the first light we turn to.*
> *Brain chemistry changes.*

Mars has many more dust devils each day than previously thought

Millions of dust devils whirl over the surface of Mars every day—geysers of vermilion powder hurled half a mile high in every direction, a dance of demons. The planet is continually popping with atmospheric instabilities. And Mars keeps making things worse. It goes into rages—huge storms kick up enough sand to turn most of the planet orange. It takes months for the air to clear.

This will play merry hell with exploration, the grime getting into spacesuits and equipment. But that's not the worst of it. Those huge storms are sucking out the last of the planet's water, sending the hydrogen of its H_2O off into the void. So there goes any hope of intelligent life ever evolving here.

> *It's a media strategy.*
> *Obscure the facts, kick up*
> *distraction. Stay orange.*

Resurfacing hypothesis proposed for Venus

It took drastic plastic surgery—a magma burst that spread
lava over wrinkles in her planetary skin, plumped up the
accumulated pocking of impact craters from a lifetime of
glancing collisions with asteroids and other meteoric but
careless lovers.

Venus spins slowly backwards from the other planets, as
if she's attempting to unspool time. Yes, she looks about
three billion years younger than she really is, but at such a
toxic cost. The surgery involved massive outgassing of CO_2,
turning her atmosphere thick, hot, unliveable. So thick that
meteors now burn up long before they ever reach her.

> *Cosmetology's*
> *revisionist history:*
> *never just skin-deep.*

Earth's gravity field detects "whistle" in Caribbean Sea

A massive current circles the Atlantic, like a clock hand sweeping round the dial. It's an inertial wave, travelling through the water's body—how the Coriolis force tries to restore balance to the disturbance caused by Earth's inexorable spinning.

The current is propelled from the African coast to the Americas, and swirls back out from the Gulf of Mexico as the Gulf Stream. It redistributes the warmth of the tropics in an attempt to return the planet's climate to balance.

In the stretch through the Caribbean Sea, where openings between brilliant islands rise from sea floor like holes in the body of a flute, the wave starts to hum a long, low note— slow, resonating pulses that human ears could never detect. But Earth's gravity field resonates in response. Sensitive instruments can record the wave peaks, recurring again and again around the dial of a year.

> *"Bleep, bleep, bleep." An SOS*
> *broadcast to the solar system—*
> *"We need help here. Over."*

Astronomer spots space rock slamming into Jupiter

There's no edge to a gas giant. No point where you could land, set your feet on a firm crust, get your bearings.

All Jupiter offers is a film of colourful cloud painted over a bombastic vapour of hydrogen and helium. It's hot down there—hot enough to melt metal—but there's probably nothing solid at the core. Only an increasingly sludgy soup. Essentially Jupiter is just big and repetitive, a wannabe star that fails to ignite. Even if it managed to suck up most of the leftovers when the sun formed, it's still not large enough to give light.

Combative moonlets and passing asteroids lob themselves, bolide bombs, at its non-surface in hopes their solid arguments will register. But nothing results. Just a flare in the toxic ammoniac fog, a brief bright spot.

The solid moons of Jupiter circle despairingly, stuck in this lesser solar system. They could sustain life, maybe. But Jupiter won't let them get away. It sulks and spins in their sky, distorting the structures of power, creating cyclones and anticyclones and more-or-less-permanent storms.

> *Voters orbit*
> *wondering how this became*
> *the centre of attention.*

Saturn's rings are disappearing

Saturn put its rings on rather late in life. After four billion years as a straightly-spherical planet moving in the sky's dark closet, something happened. Perhaps a centaur galloping between planets was captured by Saturn's gravity and exploded. Or maybe it was a slower, almost invisible development, ice fragments hooking up, their momentum shaping them into that bright spinning waltz we can see clear across the solar system—moonlets swinging within those intricate rings like pearls.

But now there's ring rain, quiet tears of regret: particles of ice being pulled from the rings towards the planet, a constant loss. Astronomers calculate they'll fade away entirely in a hundred million years or so—a mere blip of bling.

> *Coming out at last, he wonders,*
> *Why did I have to wait so long*
> *when there's so little time?*

On Neptune, it's raining diamonds

Investigators suspect that Neptune hoards enormous quantities of diamond around its core.

Neptune, so far-off and inscrutable that it does not glimmer on the human eye. We need telescopes to see its dim cobalt disc. But there's a surprising amount of substance in the distant vaults of the ice giants—Neptune and its brother baron, Uranus.

Neptune's rock heart is surrounded by the lightest elements—hydrogen, helium, nitrogen—with whiffs of methane and ammonia. But when you've amassed a layer twenty thousand kilometres thick, gravity takes over. Methane's carbon gets squeezed so hard it forms diamond crystals that sink towards the planet's centre. They may form a solid sheath, or perhaps great diamond-bergs drifting in a semi-solid sea.

We can't prove it yet. Neptune circles in an unprobed jurisdiction. But there's a trail of evidence: certain chemical signatures in spectroscopes, a suspicious amount of heat out there where it shouldn't be. And the basic physics—we know what tends to happen when enough mass is gathered up.

> *Wealth accumulates*
> *out there, beyond the taxman's*
> *equalizing eye.*

Subsurface ocean may be hiding beneath Pluto's heart

Tiny planet, largest heart—a huge bloom incised on Pluto's pinkish skin. It's a crater, a cardiac whack from an accidental asteroid on its selfish passage. Afterwards the crater filled slowly with nitrogen ice, piling in, packing in—a massive plaster on the cracked crust. The wound's accumulated weight kept tugging until Pluto swivelled on her slippery core—that liquid interior which keeps her round and tender—to stay facing her biggest, most demanding moon.

Some gravitational habit
keeps her heart attracted
to the wrong kind of man.

Comet Catalina to leave solar system after a final pass by Earth

Comet Catalina cruises past us like a passenger staring out the window on a coach tour. It's making a swing through the inner planets after starting out from the Oort Cloud—that enormously distant globe of icy chunks that marks the rim of our solar system. Catalina felt the gravitational tug of wanderlust, signed on for the tour—the kind of expedition where highlights of exotic locales are pointed out from a comfortable distance.

Other comets might come back again, cycle after cycle, like snowbirds visiting the same beach every winter until the locals start to know them. But Catalina will come by only once, a single swing round the sun, a pale, anonymous face smudged against the sky-window. Its green tail winks quickly at us, like a camera flash. It won't be back. Ever.

> *One more item ticked*
> *off the bucket list. What to post next*
> *on the photo feed?*

Zinnia becomes first flower to bloom on space station

The first zinnia ever to flower on the International Space Station hovers in the microgravity of the observational cupola. Windows on all sides and above. The zinnia turns its saffron profile to the sky, where Earth's blue limb curves at the edge of the glass. The planet and the plant float against the dark of space.

Zinnia belongs to the sunflower tribe, its roots tangled in the brilliant evolutionary braid between petal and pollinator. Like its *Helianthus* relatives, zinnias lift their sturdy faces to the sun's arc across the sky. But the space-station zinnia is spun dizzily through sixteen sunrises every day. The only slow and constant curve is the edge of that sky-blue planet below.

This bloom has been grown here from seed, tended by its latest pollinators—the humans for whom it is a precursor to future plants that will be raised up here for food. Before we travel farther out to space, we must be able to supply ourselves continuously with nourishment. And before ever there is fruit, there must be flower.

> *In the language of flowers,*
> *the zinnia expresses*
> *"thoughts of absent friends."*

End times 6:
Changing altitudes

In the northern latitudes
there comes a day, mid-August,
when you know that summer's ending.
A changing altitude
      of light, as Earth commits
to the swift, long-sided edge
      of its ellipse.

Two weeks ago, you thought
this summer's warmth could not
      possibly last long enough
and shivered in faint terror
      at its brevity.

Now suddenly you think,
How many blooms
      have taken turns
under the circling sun.
      Tiny squills. The pink
of small crabapple trees
along the streets, like little girls
who hold bouquets
at a bridal. The may-day petals
shedding like confetti.

Lilac, iris,
philadelphus billowing,
the flush of hardy roses.
Daylilies and the tallness
of hollyhock and helianthus.
The curve to starry asters
yet to come.

Each flowering time so short,
        it seemed. Yet now,
in memory, they are eternal,
as the young in yellowed photographs
are always there, and young.

And you feel there's been so much,
        your hands full of days
when the light never stopped,
so complete with scents and bees.
You think how long it's been
since the robins built their nests
        this year. So much.

And yes, you feel. Yes.
        It was enough.

Notes and sources

Epigraphs

"Samuel Pepys"

In his diary entry for May 5, 1667, nearly a year after the Great Fire of London in September 1666, Pepys comments that there have been fires in one place or other almost ever since, "as if there was a fate over people for fire." Available online at https://www.pepysdiary.com/diary/1666/09/

"Ammianus Marcellinus"

The epigraph comes from the concluding paragraph of Ammianus' *Res Gestae*, as translated by John C. Rolfe (1935). Available online at http://penelope.uchicago.edu/Thayer/E/Roman/Texts/Ammian/31*.html

"A fate for fire"

The boreal forest rings the planet's northern continents, making up almost a third of the planet's forested areas and sequestering as much carbon as the tropical forests. Fire is a natural part of the boreal ecology and, in fact, is part of the process through which carbon is extracted from the atmosphere and stored in soil. However, warming global climate (happening disproportionately in the North) is causing more frequent and intense fires, which tend to release that stored carbon into the atmosphere as CO_2.

Edward Struzik's book *Firestorm: How Wildfire Will Shape Our Future* (Island Press, 2017) provided valuable information about the disastrous Fort McMurray fire in 2016, as well as background on research and firefighting across North America.

The Norse mythology used throughout the poem comes from two principal sources: The quote from *Beowulf* that opens this poem comes from the translation by Frederick Rebsamen (HarperCollins, 1991). His translation preserves the Anglo-Saxon alliterative verse form of the original, which was composed in the 10th century by a now-unknown writer. In that epic, the warrior (later king) Beowulf faces three monsters, and the last is the fire-dragon disturbed by the theft of a single cup. That battle leads to Beowulf's death. The episodes about Thor and Loki in Jötunheim and the death of Baldr were recorded in the 12th century by Icelandic historian and poet Snorri Sturluson in a compilation of older myths known as *The Prose Edda*.

The narratives in *Beowulf* and *The Prose Edda* reflect the vanishing world views of northern, pre-Christian areas of Europe, which were very different from the Christian division of the world into heaven above, with hell below and the human world in between. The Aesir, with their home in Asgard, are powerful beings, but not gods like the omniscient, omnipresent Christian deity. The *jötnar* (generally translated as "giants") are not simply large beings or monsters—they are the cosmic forces that lie beyond both people and gods. They are occasionally helpful, but ultimately stronger than the Aesir or humans.

The actions of the Aesir—according to the apocalyptic narrative of *The Prose Edda*—ultimately provoke the *jötnar* into the conflict that leads to Ragnarok. ("Ragnarok" derives from Old Norse and means the gods' fate or judgement.) This final battle will begin with the giant Surtur, who guards the fiery realm of Muspell and will carry his bright flame-sword into the battle that leads to the ruination of Asgard.

The description of bison dying in the aftermath of fire was recorded in 1804 by Alexander Henry (cited in "The 'Grass

Fire Era' on the southeastern Canadian Prairies," by W. F. Rannie in *Prairie Perspectives* 4, 2001).

Thanks to David Jón Fuller for his counsel on the spelling of Norse names used in this poem. The poet's final choices here are a mixture of (primarily) modernized spellings with a few older variants.

"Knife on snow"

Ammianus Marcellinus (c. 330–395) lived at a time when the Roman Empire was splitting into eastern and western sections. The surviving sections of his history, called *Res Gestae,* provide vivid details of the military campaigns in which he fought, and the personalities of the rulers who came to power between 353 and 378. His favourite ruler was clearly Julian, with whom he served personally for Julian's three-year reign as emperor.

The Roman Empire in western Europe was effectively ended by the invasion of Rome by Gothic tribes in 410. This was early in the Migration Period, four centuries characterized by widespread movement of Germanic, Slavic, and Asian peoples into and around Europe.

The Weimar Republic was established after WWI, when a new constitution was adopted for Germany, establishing it as a republic rather than a monarchy. An optimistic document, it was modelled on aspects of the United States Constitution, establishing democracy and universal suffrage, and protecting individual rights. The republic ended after only fifteen years with the rise of the Nazi government.

"Manitou Asinîy" is one of the names of the Manitou Stone, which has also been called "child who fell from the sky." This iron meteorite is sacred to Indigenous people of Alberta. It is currently housed in the Royal Alberta Museum in Edmonton. Approximate pronunciation of the Cree *asinîy* ("rock") is UH-sin-ee. More information can be found online at the Royal

Alberta Museum, https://royalalbertamuseum.ca/cultural-studies/indigenous-studies/manitou-asiniy

"End times 3: Bless my eyes"
The human eye essentially operates like a camera obscura—the "pinhole" of the iris lets light into the dark chamber behind and casts an upside-down image on the screen of the retina opposite. The visual cortex of the brain corrects the reversal, so we are not aware of it.

"Path integral"
This title is a mathematical term for a technique used in many fields of physics. A path integral is a way of summing up all possible paths that could contribute to the solution of an equation—in other words, a way of simplifying calculations.

The last Ediacarans
In the Flinders Ranges of South Australia, a bronze disc is plugged into a layer of rock and engraved with the word "EDIACARAN" (approximate pronunciation: eed-e-AH-car-an). This is a geologists' "golden spike," marking a point where we can see the planet's history shift. This rock began as sediment laid down on the seabed margins of an ancient supercontinent, Rodinia, at a time when almost all the world's landmass was connected and surrounded by a continuous ocean, Panthalassa.

The discontinuity is clear to see. Below the disc, dim purple stone is evidence of massive glaciations worldwide—the Cryogenian period. Above it lie tawny slabs of cap carbonate. Their chemistry tells the story of global change, a rapid and radical warming. Within this layer of rock are fossils of the mysterious "Ediacaran biota," some of the oldest evidence of animal life. These creatures don't look like anything that survives today. They resembled quill pens, quilted cushions, pasta tubes, their shapes preserved in the sponge-like microbial mats in which they fed.

At the upper end of the cap carbonate layer, the rocks' chemistry changes and Ediacaran life forms abruptly end. Layers of black shale suggest that a loss of dissolved oxygen suffocated the environment in which the Ediacaran animals lived.

Rodinia broke up and the deposits of cap carbonate were carried around the world on the shoulders of moving continental plates. Today, in the Yangtze Gorges, thick layers of that rock hold many Ediacaran fossils. In the upper, most recent layers, these include a worm-like creature, *Yilingia spiciformis* (approximate pronunciation: Yi-LING-ia SPICE-i-formis). One such specimen includes a mortichnium, making it one of the rare fossils where an animal leaves the track of its movement just before death.

"7. Tales of the apocalypse"

In Old Norse mythology, *Naglfar* (approximate pronunciation: Nal-far) is the largest ship in the world, held in Muspell, the realm of the fire giants. It is made from the accumulated fingernails and toenails of the dead. When the sea floods in before the last battle between gods and giants, *Naglfar* will be loosened to float.

"10. _Ideonella sakaiensis_"

Ideonella sakaiensis (approximate pronunciation: EYE-dyon-EL-a SAK-eye-en-sis) is a microbe discovered in 2015 in a Japanese recycling facility. The microbe has already evolved a capacity to break down PET molecules. Decomposition is likely the most important function of microbes in every ecosystem, in an ongoing cycle of growth, breakdown, and rebuilding that restores nutrients to the environment.

"11. After Ragnarok"

The Old Norse myth of Ragnarok is one of numerous apocalyptic narratives found in cultures around the world. In this one, two humans will survive the destruction by hiding in the wood known as Hoddmímis holt.

Travels in the solar system

The titles in this series of _haibun_ (a form consisting of prose passages followed by haiku) are drawn from quirkier headlines in the daily Sigma Xi SmartBrief e-newsletter.

"'Planet nine is out there,' claim astronomers"

One possible explanation for anomalies in the solar system's orbits—put forward by Caltech astronomers Konstantin Batygin and Mike Brown—is a large planet ejected from the early planetary line-up and continuing to orbit the sun at a much greater distance. https://solarsystem.nasa.gov/planets/hypothetical-planet-x/in-depth/

"Tiny collisions shape Mercury's atmosphere"

The planet Mercury circles the sun twice for every three rotations on its own axis. As a result, a "day" (from one sunrise to the next) lasts two years.

"Subsurface ocean may be hiding beneath Pluto's heart"
Pluto's moon, Charon, is half the size of the planet itself—the largest moon relative to its planet in the solar system. Tidal interactions have synchronized the orbital periods between the two bodies so that the same hemisphere of Pluto always faces Charon.

Acknowledgements

I am grateful for so much help and support in the writing and publishing of *Knife on Snow*. My gratitude goes out to:

- Sharon, Jamis, and Melissa at Turnstone Press for welcoming me to the press and bringing the manuscript to book form.
- John Wall Barger for stimulating editorial discussions.
- Poet and Indigenous knowledge-holder Naomi McIlwraith for her generosity in reading *Knife on Snow* through an Indigenous lens.
- Melissa Morrow for her thorough and thoughtful proofreading.
- John Vogel for turning "Path integral" into an amazing video poem for the *Talking Writing* website (https:// talkingwriting.com/video-path-integral). "Subsurface ocean may be hiding beneath Pluto's heart" and "Zinnia becomes first flower to bloom on space station" have also appeared in that online magazine.
- The editors of the Westmount Community League's newsletter, who requested the poem which became "Your house may be eligible for a heritage plaque." However big its aspirations, poetry is ultimately local.
- The active, diverse, and evolving writing community here in Edmonton, which welcomed me four decades ago and has been an inspiration and support system ever since.
- This land where I found myself, the territory now known as Treaty Six, where people have been creating songs and stories for at least eight thousand years.
- This planet, which sustains us all.
- And finally, my dearest David. Always.

Alice Major emigrated from Scotland at the age of eight, and grew up in Toronto before coming west to work as a weekly newspaper reporter in central British Columbia. She has lived in Edmonton, Alberta since 1981.

Knife on Snow is her 12th collection of poetry. Like her poetry, her essay collection, *Intersecting Sets: A Poet Looks at Science,* is inspired by a lifelong love of science, from physics and geology to evolution and cognitive science. Her work has appeared in dozens of literary magazines and other publications, as well as more than 20 anthologies. She has given hundreds of readings across Canada as well as in the UK, Australia and the U.S., and has received multiple awards for her writing, including the Lieutenant Governor of Alberta Distinguished Artist Award.

Alice is also known as a community builder. She has served as president of the Writers Guild of Alberta, chair of the Edmonton Arts Council and past president of the League of Canadian Poets. She was appointed to a two-year term as the first poet laureate for the City of Edmonton and founded the Edmonton Poetry Festival, now in its 18th year. In November, 2019, she received an honorary doctorate of letters from the University of Alberta.